Original title:
Beyond Attraction

Author: Johan Kirsipuu
ISBN HARDBACK: 978-9916-89-031-8
ISBN PAPERBACK: 978-9916-89-032-5
ISBN EBOOK: 978-9916-89-033-2

Veils of Magnetic Possibility

In shadows dance the dreams we crave,
A flicker of light, a heart's brave wave.
Each whisper pulls like gravity's thread,
Binding our souls, where hope is fed.

Through midnight skies, our wishes soar,
Chasing the stars from shore to shore.
In silence, love ignites a spark,
Illuminating the hidden dark.

Echoes of Unseen Connections

Threads of fate weave in unseen streams,
Dancing identities, intertwined dreams.
Each heartbeat sings a resonant theme,
In the sacred space where souls redeem.

Whispers of truth in crowded halls,
Silent responses to destiny's calls.
Underneath layers, life subtly links,
In the tapestry, our essence winks.

The Allure of Uncharted Paths

Unmapped trails beckon with silent grace,
Luring the brave to an unfamiliar place.
Each step unfolds like a blooming flower,
Revealing joys in nature's power.

Beneath the trees, where shadows blend,
A chance encounter, a newfound friend.
In the wild, where spirits ignite,
Every corner holds a spark of light.

Whispers in the Windows of Desire

Behind glass panes, secrets reside,
Glimmers of longing that hearts can't hide.
Yearning glances through the night's embrace,
Shadows dance in a soft, sweet space.

Each heartbeat echoes, a tender sigh,
As stories unfold beneath the sky.
In the silence, our wishes align,
Painting desires in intimate design.

The Existence of What Lies Ahead

In the mist where shadows play,
Dreams awaken, night to day.
Unseen doors await the bold,
Whispers of stories yet untold.

Winds of change begin to stir,
Hope ignites, a gentle purr.
With each step, horizons bend,
Towards the light where paths transcend.

Hues of Desirability in the Dusk

The sky blushes with evening's call,
Softened shades begin to fall.
Silhouettes dance on fading light,
Desires bloom within the night.

Crimson whispers on the breeze,
Every moment aims to please.
Hearts entwine in twilight's glow,
In the dusk, true colors flow.

Fragments of Attraction's Infinity

Scattered stars in cosmic play,
Pulling hearts in every way.
Infinite sparks ignite the soul,
Binding threads that make us whole.

Echoes linger, soft and sweet,
In the rhythm of our heartbeat.
Fragments weave a tapestry bright,
Guiding lovers through the night.

The Path of Unseen Undercurrents

Beneath the surface, currents flow,
Whispers carry tales we know.
Hidden paths weave through the dark,
Every turn ignites a spark.

Like a river, life will bend,
Trust the journey, not the end.
In unseen realms, we find our way,
Guided gently, come what may.

Tides of Implicit Connection

Whispers ride the silent breeze,
Hearts in sync, as if at ease.
A glance exchanged, a fleeting spark,
Lost in thought, beneath the dark.

Moonlit nights bring forth the glow,
Unspoken bonds that ebb and flow.
In shadows deep, our spirits merge,
A hidden force, an unseen urge.

Threading Through the Unconscious

Dreams entwined, a dance of fate,
Through winding paths, we navigate.
Silent echoes in the night,
Whispers guide us, taking flight.

Threads of thought, we pull and weave,
In this tapestry, we believe.
Subtle signs in every glance,
Unravel secrets in the trance.

Layers of Unfamiliar Warmth

Gentle touch, a feathery sigh,
In this world, we learn to fly.
Like sun-kissed mornings, fresh and bright,
New emotions spark the light.

Wrapped in layers, soft and deep,
Unfamiliar warmth, yet mine to keep.
Each heartbeat sings a tender song,
Silent rhythms where we belong.

The Depths of Subtle Infatuation

Eyes meet softly, a fleeting glance,
Caught in moments, lost in chance.
A hidden smile, a shy retreat,
Each word lingers, bittersweet.

In quiet spaces, feelings bloom,
Softened shadows, love in bloom.
Unraveled threads of passion grow,
Though unconfessed, we both know.

Enigmatic Pull of The Unsaid

In shadows where whispers dwell,
Words unspoken weave their spell.
Beneath the gaze, a story glows,
The heart knows what silence shows.

Questions linger in the air,
Silence thick, like muted flare.
Each pause holds a sacred truth,
In stillness lies ageless youth.

A glance exchanged, a spark ignites,
In uncharted depths, the night invites.
The thrill of what could be unfolds,
In realms of secrets still untold.

Secrets in the Space Between

In the breath before a sigh,
A universe tucked, oh so shy.
Between the lines of what we say,
Lies a dance that sways away.

Not all is shared in the light,
Some dreams flourish out of sight.
Hidden truths like stars alight,
Twinkling softly in the night.

We navigate this silent map,
Each heartbeat strumming, a gentle tap.
In the void, connection grows,
A tapestry only we can sew.

When Hearts Almost Touch

A heartbeat dances in the space,
Two souls meeting at a pace.
Fingers brush like fleeting light,
In the hush, pure magic's right.

Eyes speak volumes, words are few,
In that moment, just me and you.
The world fades, it’s us alone,
In this silence, we've both grown.

Hope hangs heavy in the air,
Fragile dreams, a whispered dare.
When hearts almost touch, time stills,
A bond forged in unseen thrills.

The Lure of Lingering Glances

In crowded rooms, I find your gaze,
A spark ignites, a silent blaze.
Lingering looks that spark the night,
In those moments, everything's right.

A fleeting smile, a subtle nod,
Two souls dance, a quiet applaud.
Lost in thoughts where dreams entwine,
In stolen moments, hearts align.

The echo of what could transpire,
Each glance fuels an unquenched fire.
In the space where we both reside,
The lure of glances, our secret guide.

When Words Fail to Describe

In the silence, feelings roam,
Whispers dance, yet stay unknown.
Chasing shadows of a thought,
Unspoken truths that can't be caught.

Eyes that speak a thousand tales,
Hope that breathes when silence pales.
Moments linger, just a glance,
In the void, we find romance.

Lost in meaning, found in sighs,
Behind each smile, a million lies.
Hearts that beat, yet none can hear,
Desires wrapped in quiet fear.

Fragments scattered, thoughts unearthed,
In the stillness, we find worth.
Memories fade yet still remain,
In the darkness, blooms the pain.

Perhaps the silence holds the key,
To unlock what’s meant to be.
When words retreat, emotions flare,
In the quiet, souls lay bare.

The Symphony of Unexplored Emotions

A melody drifts through the air,
Carrying dreams beyond despair.
Notes that whisper of what could be,
Echoing hopes, wild and free.

Strings that bridge the heart's divide,
Beats that pulse with joy and pride.
In every chord, a tale untold,
A dance of feelings, brave and bold.

Uncharted depths of love and loss,
Each vibration speaks, no matter the cost.
In the crescendo, fears ignite,
Yet in the fade, there's gentle light.

Fingers reach for stars unseen,
In the quiet, we dance between.
A symphony of souls, apart,
Yet intertwined, heart to heart.

Let the music guide us through,
To realms where dreams are born anew.
In unexplored, we find our song,
A harmony where we belong.

Sketches of Something More

Pencil lines on faded sheets,
Drawn in hopes, where longing meets.
Fragments of a distant dream,
In each stroke, a silent scream.

Shapes that hint at what could be,
Visions wrapped in mystery.
Colors blend yet fade away,
A canvas waits for light of day.

Shadows swim in twilight's glow,
Sketches dance on hearts that know.
Echoes of a whispered prayer,
In the margins, love lays bare.

Each eraser pulls the thread,
Of stories unsaid, paths we tread.
Beneath the surface, feelings soar,
Yearning for something more, much more.

So we draw, though hearts may ache,
In every line, a choice we make.
Chasing shadows, we explore,
Sketching out a distant shore.

A Canvas Yet to Be Painted

Blank and waiting for the dawn,
Colors mix, yet feel withdrawn.
On this canvas, dreams can stretch,
What awaits? A life to sketch.

Brushstrokes tremble, hearts align,
Hues of hope with drops of wine.
Each splash tells of joy and sorrow,
Creating tales to fill tomorrow.

Shapes emerge from empty space,
A whisper of a soft embrace.
In each corner, stories hide,
A journey felt, a life applied.

Fingers poised to make their mark,
In the quiet, ignites a spark.
Every splash, a heartbeat's call,
On this canvas, we find our all.

So let the colors boldly flow,
In vibrant waves, our spirits grow.
With every layer, life unfurls,
As we paint our dreams in swirls.

Threads of Intrigue and Infinity

In whispers soft, the secrets weave,
A tapestry of dreams to believe.
With every stitch, a story spun,
In shadows deep, where time is none.

The colors dance, entwined and bright,
Reflecting hopes in the fading light.
Each thread a path, a choice to make,
Connections forged, no chance to break.

Unravelled tales of distant lands,
Exploring hearts with open hands.
The fabric pulls, a gentle sway,
Inviting souls to come and play.

What lies beyond, we cannot see,
Yet in this web, we find the key.
Through laughter, tears, and silent glances,
We journey forth, as fate advances.

Together woven, tightly bound,
In every silence, love is found.
Through threads of life, we intertwine,
A delicate art, both yours and mine.

Dancing in the Shadows of Affection

Beneath the moon, soft whispers sway,
With every heartbeat, night holds sway.
In shadows deep, where secrets play,
We twirl as one, in sweet ballet.

The gentle breeze, it calls our names,
In hushed tones, we ignite the flames.
With every glance, a story flows,
In unison, our passion grows.

The world stands still, as if to pause,
Captured in this dance without cause.
A rhythm shared, two souls align,
In twilight's grasp, where stars entwine.

Through echoes soft, our laughter rings,
Embraced by night, we find our wings.
The shadows wrap, a tender cloak,
In silent vows, our hearts invoke.

In every twirl, our fears released,
In this embrace, we feel the beast.
For in the dark, our spirits soar,
Dancing together, forevermore.

The Symphony of Silent Pulls

A gentle tug beneath the skin,
An unspoken bond where love begins.
In quiet notes, emotions rise,
A symphony played beneath the skies.

With every glance, our hearts align,
In silent pulls, a love divine.
Melodies swirl, unseen and clear,
A cadence formed, keeping us near.

The orchestra of hearts ignites,
In whispered tones, we find our rights.
Each string a promise, strong yet light,
As twilight fades, we shine bright.

In unison, our spirits soar,
Through whispered winds, we crave for more.
An echo lingers, sweet and true,
By subtle signs, I’m drawn to you.

United souls, through time and space,
In the quiet, we find our place.
A symphony that never ends,
In silent pulls, our love transcends.

Currents of Enigmatic Entwinement

In flowing tides, our fates align,
In currents deep, your heart is mine.
With every wave, a question stirs,
What lies beneath, in whispered murmurs?

The water sings of tales untold,
Of lovers' paths, both young and old.
Entwined like roots in soil so firm,
We dance among the waves, we squirm.

In unseen depths, a spark ignites,
Together lost in starry nights.
The currents pull us ever near,
In ocean's heart, we know no fear.

Through tempest storms and tranquil seas,
Our bond, a compass, strong as breeze.
In the abyss, we find our truth,
In the dance of waves, we reclaim our youth.

Forever swirling, deep and wide,
In currents of fate, we shall abide.
For every ebb, there’s flow anew,
In enigmatic love, I cling to you.

Navigating the Waters of Desire

Beneath a shimmering sea of dreams,
Waves of passion gently sway.
Hearts adrift in silken beams,
Guided by the stars' soft play.

Whispers echo on the breeze,
Tides pull us closer still.
In secret coves, we find our ease,
Chasing shadows, bent to thrill.

The compass spins with every gaze,
Uncharted paths to explore.
Lost in a fervent, lingering haze,
We drift from the familiar shore.

Each touch ignites the midnight air,
With fervor that cannot cease.
In every glance, a silent dare,
Yearning for a sweet release.

Together we sail through longing's night,
Our hearts a map, so true.
In the depths of an endless flight,
Navigating me and you.

Glancing at the Edge of Reality

In twilight's hush, the shadows blend,
Where dreams and truth collide.
A fragile line where moments bend,
On the brink, we dare to ride.

Fleeting glimpses of what might be,
Colors clash in fleeting hues.
Reality's dance, a mystery,
Where nothing is left to lose.

Eyes wide open to the sky,
Catching rays of a distant sun.
Here, the impossible can fly,
And worlds within us run.

We chase the whispers of the dawn,
With hearts that pulse and race.
In an embrace where hope is drawn,
Straddling space and time and grace.

Moments shimmer, then dissolve,
Like fog at break of day.
In this dance, we both resolve,
To find our own true way.

The Pulse of an Unforeseen Dance

Beneath the moon's soft, silver gaze,
We twirl on this midnight stage.
In rhythms found in ocean waves,
A spark ignites a new age.

Each heartbeat flows with possibility,
Echoes of what lies ahead.
Steps in time with sincerity,
A dance where silence is spread.

Hands entwine in fateful grasp,
Spinning stories wind and weave.
Lost in the moment, we clasp,
In what our souls believe.

Around us, galaxies collide,
As stars shimmer in our eyes.
An unforeseen joy, we guide,
In harmony, we rise.

Through the alleys of fate's embrace,
We leap into the unknown.
Through the pulse of a timeless space,
In this dance, we have grown.

Beyond Words of Hidden Longing

In the silence where secrets bloom,
Whispers dance on the edge of night.
Words can hardly pierce the gloom,
Yet hearts can feel the light.

A glance exchanged, it speaks so clear,
In every sigh, a silent plea.
In this realm of dreams held dear,
We find our truth, we find our key.

Deep inside, the fires burn bright,
Drawing forth what lies beneath.
In hidden longing, we take flight,
A tapestry of belief.

Each pulse, a promise yet unspun,
Each breath, an echo of desire.
Together, we'll awaken the sun,
As we dance in love's attire.

Beyond the words, the silence sings,
A language only we can know.
In the fabric of what longing brings,
Our souls entwined will flow.

Whispers of Unseen Threads

In twilight's hush, secrets soar,
Beneath the stars, they gently explore.
Soft murmurs weave through the night,
Binding souls in dimmest light.

Echoes of warmth brush through the air,
Unseen threads, a dance we share.
Fingers trace what hearts can't speak,
In silence, the bond feels unique.

Dreams flutter like restless wings,
A tapestry of unspoken things.
Each glance a spark, a fleeting glow,
In shadows where hidden feelings grow.

When skies surrender to the dawn,
Awakening hopes, softly drawn.
With every sigh, the world ignites,
A symphony of whispered flights.

In the weave of time, we find our way,
Threads entwined in this delicate play.
Whispers linger, holding tight,
Unseen threads, guiding us through the night.

Echoes of Silent Closeness

In the quiet, hearts resonate,
An unbroken bond we cultivate.
Silence speaks in tender ways,
Filling the space with gentle praise.

Eyes meet like stars that align,
A universe wrapped in design.
No words needed, just a glance,
In the stillness, we find our dance.

Time slows down, moments extend,
With unvoiced feelings that transcend.
Each heartbeat is a melody,
In the calm, just you and me.

The world fades to a distant hum,
To this rhythm, we both succumb.
A whisper shared, a breath of fate,
In the silence, we celebrate.

In the embrace of the unseen air,
Echoes linger, soft and rare.
In every pause, a promise made,
In silent closeness, love won't fade.

Shadows of Unspoken Longing

Under the veil of the moon's soft glow,
Whispers of longing, we both know.
In shadows cast by fleeting light,
Hidden desires long for flight.

Glances dance like fireflies at dusk,
With every heartbeat, we're lost in trust.
Words unsaid hang heavily still,
In the silence, there's too much thrill.

The night's embrace holds secrets tight,
Yearnings echo, banishing fright.
Every corner, a place we dream,
In shadows of thought, love will teem.

Unsung wishes float on the breeze,
Carried forth with such gentle ease.
Longing deep as the ocean wide,
In silent shadows, we confide.

As dawn approaches, the dreams retreat,
Yet in the heart, they still compete.
Unspoken longings may fade away,
But their shadows in memory will stay.

Dance of the Unfamiliar Heart

In the stillness, a rhythm starts,
A hesitant sway of unfamiliar hearts.
Footsteps falter, but courage grows,
In the dance, a new story flows.

Eyes meet in a delicate trance,
Caught unawares by daring chance.
With each beat, the world aligns,
In tandem, a spark of the divine.

Uncharted paths guide our way,
Through twists and turns where shadows play.
Every movement, a fearless embark,
In the world of the unknown, we spark.

A melody wraps around our souls,
As time unveils its wondrous goals.
Swaying softly to fate's design,
In this dance, our hearts entwine.

As the night wanes, the music fades,
Yet the spirit of the dance cascades.
Though paths may part, the echoes remain,
In the dance of hearts, love's sweet refrain.

Echoes of a Shared Silence

In the stillness, whispers play,
Two hearts beating, soft and shy.
Memories linger, dusk til day,
In the shadows, questions lie.

Lost in thoughts, where dreams collide,
A bond unspoken, yet so clear.
In silence, worlds begin to hide,
The echoes holding all we fear.

Through the night, the stars align,
Silent tales of love retold.
Hand in hand, a gentle sign,
Two souls woven, brave and bold.

In moments shared, we find our way,
Each glance a promise, soft and warm.
In this silence, we shall stay,
Together weathering the storm.

As dawn approaches, light breaks free,
The silence sings, our truth unfolds.
Forever in this harmony,
Our hearts, a tapestry of gold.

Untangling the Web of Desire

In shadows cast by fleeting dreams,
Desire dances, wild and free.
With every breath, the longing beams,
Across the vastness, you and me.

Threads of passion, interlace,
A delicate dance of give and take.
In every touch, a tender grace,
Awakening what’s yet to wake.

Beneath the surface, secrets churn,
The fire ignites with silent flames.
In every glance, we yearn and learn,
Unraveling whispered, hidden names.

As tangled webs, we weave and spin,
Caught in the pull of fate's embrace.
A thrilling game where none can win,
Yet here we stand, our hearts in place.

With every sigh and breath we take,
Desire's path unclear and bright.
In every moment, choices make,
Two souls entwined, igniting light.

Fragments of Intertwined Souls

Beneath the surface, echoes blend,
Two lives crossing, fates collide.
In each fragment, stories send,
A tapestry of love and pride.

In every glance, a spark ignites,
Intertwined in cosmic dance.
Through endless days, through quiet nights,
Our souls partake in fate's romance.

What once was whole, now gently frays,
Yet beauty blooms in every tear.
Through tangled paths and endless ways,
We find the strength to persevere.

The world around us fades away,
In sacred space, we find our ground.
With every heartbeat, come what may,
In fragments, wholeness must be found.

Together, we are woven tight,
In every fading, bruised embrace.
For in the dark, we sense the light,
Our intertwined souls find their place.

The Allure of the Uncharted

In the distance, horizons call,
Oceans vast with tales untold.
Every sunrise, shadows fall,
Adventures wait for hearts so bold.

With maps that lead to dreams unknown,
We step beyond our comfort zone.
In every challenge, seeds are sown,
A longing deep, a wish to roam.

The path uncertain, yet we ride,
With courage drawn from love and trust.
In open skies, our fears subside,
To chase the dawn, we feel we must.

Through valleys low and mountains high,
Every stumble, a lesson learned.
The stars our guide, the endless sky,
In the uncharted, we return.

Together, we embrace the quest,
Hearts alight with wanderlust.
In every moment, life's a test,
To find our truth, in dreams we trust.

Surreal Landscapes of Unexpected Desire

In shadows cast by twilight's veil,
Mountains sway like whispered tales.
Waves of color blend and twist,
Dreams unfold in a painter's mist.

Fields of gold beneath the moon,
Echoes sing a breathless tune.
Cypress trees in gentle dance,
Invite the heart to take a chance.

Mirrors glisten, worlds collide,
In these depths, our souls confide.
Starlit paths to nowhere lead,
Awaken hope, ignite the seed.

Rivers flow with liquid light,
Carving truths in endless night.
Horizon bends, the sky ignites,
In surreal dreams, desire writes.

Surreal landscapes, lost in gaze,
Where time contorts in fleeting ways.
Each brushstroke speaks of tender fire,
Awakening our hidden desire.

The Essence of Unfamiliar Warmth

Beneath the veil of morning's glow,
Hearts awaken, spirits flow.
Gentle whispers ride the breeze,
Carrying secrets through the trees.

Fingers brush where shadows meet,
Silk and velvet, soft retreat.
In the silence, love ignites,
Familiar warmth amidst the nights.

Sunrise captures moments rare,
With each heartbeat, love laid bare.
Uncharted realms, where feelings soar,
The essence calls, we crave for more.

Tangled webs of soft embrace,
Slide into the unknown space.
Finding comfort in the strange,
A tender spark that feels like change.

In laughter shared, we find our ground,
In every breath, our hearts unbound.
The warmth we seek, though unfamiliar,
Binds us close, a sweet distiller.

Tides that Pull while Keeping Distance

Moonlit waves that kiss the shore,
Draw us close, yet want for more.
Distance measured by the tide,
Yearning hearts that cannot hide.

Voices carried on the swell,
Softly weaving tales to tell.
Waves retreat, then crash anew,
In this rhythm, love breaks through.

Echoed laughter in the foam,
Lingers where we feel at home.
Yet the sea keeps us apart,
With every pulse, it breaks the heart.

Celestial dance of light and dark,
Pulls us in, leaves little mark.
A push and pull of dreams and doubt,
In every wave, we scream and shout.

Reflections lost in azure grace,
Navigating through time and space.
Tides that pull yet keep us free,
In the distance, you reach for me.

Heartstrings Touched by Intangible Threads

Invisible binds that softly tug,
Through silent spaces, warm and snug.
Each pulse a whisper in the night,
Connecting souls with tender light.

Fingers dance on fragile air,
Crafting bonds beyond compare.
Threads of longing, woven tight,
In the shadows, dreams ignite.

Moments slip like grains of sand,
Yet we grasp with gentle hands.
Held together by the unseen,
In this world, we drift between.

Heartstrings strummed by fate's own hand,
Play a tune we understand.
In the depths of quiet sighs,
Intangible love never dies.

Weaving stories in the dark,
Every glance a fleeting spark.
In the silence, hearts will tread,
Drawn together, love is bred.

Dreams Woven in Unfamiliar Light

In twilight hues, dreams take flight,
Soft whispers weave through the night.
Unseen paths beckon, oh so bright,
Promises dance in the fading light.

Shadows shift with the evening breeze,
Hidden hopes sway like the trees.
Each flicker of stars, a tease,
A tapestry of heart's unease.

The lanterns glow, casting their spell,
Where secrets whisper, there stories dwell.
In the depths of night, we rebel,
Chasing the dreams only time can tell.

Through veils of mist, our spirits soar,
In unfamiliar light, we explore.
Fears dissolve, we crave for more,
A journey inward, forevermore.

Each dawn unveils a brand new start,
With woven dreams, we find our part.
United by light, we are not apart,
In the grandeur of night, we share one heart.

The Fathomless Depth of Her Gaze

In her gaze, stories unfold,
Tales of warmth and secrets bold.
A ocean's depth, a sight to behold,
In her eyes, the universe is told.

Stars shimmer bright in sapphire seas,
Whispers linger on midnight breeze.
Every glance brings us to our knees,
Her silent strength, a soft unease.

Time stands still, moments entwine,
In her presence, all hearts align.
With just a look, pathways define,
Infinite worlds, in love, we find.

Between the silk of calm and storm,
Her eyes reflect the heart’s true form.
With every blink, warm thoughts swarm,
In their depth, we feel the warm.

A precious balance, fierce and tame,
Each glance ignites a hidden flame.
Her depths, a puzzle without a name,
In the silence, we play our game.

Unraveled Desires Under Starry Skies

Beneath the canopy, wishes gleam,
Unraveled desires in twilight's dream.
Each flicker of light pulls at the seam,
Hearts awaken in a hopeful beam.

The cosmos whispers, secrets shared,
In the quiet night, souls laid bare.
With every star, we are prepared,
To catch the dreams we long declared.

Night blooms softly, shadows align,
Within the silence, hearts intertwine.
Among the stars, love feels divine,
In deep connection, all fears decline.

We dance with echoes of starlit grace,
Lost in the moment, we find our place.
Every heartbeat, a gentle embrace,
Under the sky, time leaves no trace.

As dawn approaches, colors embrace,
Wishes linger, love's warm trace.
In the glow of day, dreams have their grace,
Unraveled desires, our hearts' safe space.

Mysteries Linger in the Air

In quiet whispers, secrets play,
Mysteries linger, night fades to gray.
Invisible threads weave tales each day,
In shadowed corners, they softly sway.

The moonlight dances, casting new shapes,
Enigmas float where the silence drapes.
With each heartbeat, the mind escapes,
In the labyrinth, our heart reshapes.

Through fog and haze, visions unfold,
Stories of old that yearn to be told.
In the spaces between, fate takes hold,
A treasure buried, worth more than gold.

With every breeze, a secret's sigh,
Echoes of dreams that forever fly.
In the stillness, forgotten hopes lie,
Mysteries linger, asking us why.

As dawn approaches, clarity blooms,
Yet in the light, still, a shadow looms.
For in every breath, the magic resumes,
Mysteries thrive in our hearts' dark rooms.

Underneath the Surface of Attraction

Eyes meet briefly, a spark ignites,
Hearts whisper softly in the night.
Unraveled secrets, yearning to be told,
Echoes of longing, a dance so bold.

Unseen currents pull us near,
Kindred souls in quiet fear.
A glance, a touch, a fleeting dream,
Underneath, a hidden stream.

Sparks of laughter, a fleeting tease,
Moments etched in timeless freeze.
What lies beneath this surface sheen?
A world concealed—both fierce and keen.

With every heartbeat, shadows sway,
In your eyes I find my way.
Together we tread the fine line,
Between what's yours and what is mine.

In the end, what will unfold?
Where this path leads remains untold.
Still I linger, drawn to you,
Beneath the surface, love anew.

Hidden Orchards of Kindred Spirits

In secret groves where whispers play,
Branches bend, swaying sway.
Fruits of laughter, sweetly shared,
Nurtured hopes we both declared.

Countless dreams in shadows hide,
A tender bond we cannot bide.
Each heartbeat like a gentle breeze,
Stirring leaves of hidden trees.

Ripened thoughts beneath the sky,
The spark that glimmers, we can't deny.
Roots entwined deep in the ground,
With every glance, our hearts unbound.

Blossoms dance in radiant light,
Two souls tethered, taking flight.
From hidden orchards, secrets born,
In unity, we won't be torn.

So let us wander, hand in hand,
Through these realms, across the land.
In the quiet, love we sow,
Where kindred spirits freely grow.

Lighthouses in the Fog of Fancy

In swirling mists, two hearts align,
A beacon's glow, so divine.
Guiding ships on their wild quest,
Through waves of doubt, we find our rest.

The harbor calls with whispered dreams,
Softly weaving, silken seams.
Flickering lights through tangled haze,
Illuminating our secret ways.

Between the tides, our passions rise,
Starlit gazes, infinite skies.
Every pulse, a rhythmic wave,
In this fog, our hearts behave.

Navigating through the unknown,
With every breath, we're not alone.
Lighthouses shine through night’s embrace,
In this journey, we find our place.

As time drifts on like moment’s tide,
In your light, I shall abide.
Together we steer through misty views,
Lighthouses guiding me to you.

Tidal Waves of Unconscious Temptation

Rising currents pull us close,
In every glance, we feel the prose.
A subtle push, a gentle pull,
Unspoken desires dance and lull.

Hidden depths of hearts obscure,
Yearnings buried, feelings pure.
With every touch, a tide ignites,
Tidal waves of whispered nights.

Cascading echoes roll and sweep,
Through secret dreams, together leap.
What lies beyond this fragile shore?
Unconscious paths we both explore.

In the stillness, passions bloom,
Lost in the depths, where shadows loom.
We're like ships caught in a storm,
Swept away, our hearts transform.

As many tides rise and fall,
Through soft murmurs, we heed the call.
In the ocean, wild and free,
Tidal waves unite you and me.

Constellations of Untold Stories

In the night sky, whispers reside,
Each star a tale, softly tied.
Forgotten dreams, woven in light,
Shining bright, out of sight.

Galaxies spin, dance and weave,
Stories eclipse, in twilight we grieve.
Unseen paths where shadows play,
Every glance, a word to say.

Winds carry secrets of the past,
Echoes of time, gentle and vast.
In constellations, we find our place,
Mapping the heart in cosmic grace.

Silent symphonies, quietly hum,
Each heartbeat in rhythm, a distant drum.
Connecting souls, a celestial thread,
Binding the living with the dead.

Under the gaze of moonlit dreams,
We gather stardust, collecting beams.
A tapestry of stories untold,
In the night sky, we find our gold.

The Pulse of Electromagnetic Hearts

In the hum of the night, we feel the beat,
Waves of energy pulse, alive and sweet.
Hearts attuned to the rhythm's dance,
In the quiet, souls find their chance.

Beneath the surface, currents flow,
Invisible ties that help us grow.
In every spark, a connection shines,
Bridging the distance between our lines.

The language of light, it calls us near,
In every heartbeat, we hold our fear.
Yet in the chaos, we hear the tune,
A symphony played by sun and moon.

Each pulse a whisper, a word of fate,
Magnetic forces cannot wait.
Together we rise like electric streams,
Chasing the shadows, embracing dreams.

In the tapestry woven, we find our role,
Carving out pathways, igniting the soul.
Together we'll dance in this cosmic art,
In the pulse of electromagnetic hearts.

Mystical Currents of Affinity

In the autumn breeze, we find our way,
Through trails of leaves, where memories play.
Whispers of fate softly intertwine,
Two souls adrift, beneath the pine.

Currents of magic, flowing so free,
Connected by threads we cannot see.
Every glance, an unspoken tie,
In the silence, our spirits fly.

The dance of shadows, light and shade,
In every heartbeat, a bond is made.
Time weaves its stories in gentle spins,
Where affinity holds, love always wins.

Through rivers of time, we drift and sway,
Finding our rhythm in the night and day.
Every moment, a precious sign,
In mystical currents, your heart and mine.

Together we wander, forever roam,
In the sanctuary of love, our home.
With every flow, our essence blends,
In mystical currents, we make amends.

In the Silence Between Heartbeats

In the stillness, time takes a breath,
Moments suspended, dancing with death.
Each heartbeat a whisper, soft as air,
In the silence, we find what's rare.

Between beats, secrets patiently lie,
In tender spaces where echoes sigh.
What goes unspoken, felt yet unseen,
Unveils the magic that lies between.

A soft connection, a fleeting glance,
In the quiet, we share our dance.
Infinite stories hidden from view,
In the spaces, it's me and you.

The clock ticks slowly, but hearts race fast,
In every silence, memories cast.
Hold me close in this gentle space,
In the silence between, we find our grace.

Forever entwined, we linger here,
List with our dreams, shading our fear.
In the heartbeat's pause, we rise above,
In the silence, we cultivate love.

Unfolding the Mystique of Attraction

A gaze can bridge two souls,
Silent whispers ignite the air.
Fingers brush, a fleeting spark,
In that moment, nothing compares.

Hearts dance in a rhythm rare,
Echoing secrets in the dark.
Unseen threads weave a tapestry,
In the glow of a single spark.

Time halts, as worlds collide,
A chemistry that's hard to fight.
Lost in thoughts of 'what could be',
A puzzle that feels just right.

Eyes that hold a thousand dreams,
Stories waiting to unfold.
In the dance of chance and fate,
Love's mystery, bold and untold.

As moments pass, hearts intertwine,
The mystique draws us near.
Each heartbeat echoes a truth,
In the space where we disappear.

Stars Aligning in Quietude

In tranquil nights, the sky unfolds,
Constellations drawn with care.
Silent wishes drift like gold,
Promising dreams that we share.

In stillness, the cosmos glows,
A gentle light that beckons us.
Moments pause, the world slows down,
In the quiet, there's a trust.

Whispers carried by the breeze,
Softly speaking to the heart.
With each twinkle, a story grows,
From the universe, we won't part.

In this space, we find our peace,
As galaxies dance in our sight.
Two hearts bound by celestial ties,
Stars aligning in the night.

In the calm, our spirits rise,
Together as shadows blend.
A love that feels like starlit skies,
In quietude, we transcend.

The Spark in the Heart's Constellation

Within the heart, a fire glows,
Drawing warmth from every beat.
Embers flicker, softly tease,
In the silence, love's heartbeat.

Like stars that dance in cosmic bliss,
Their light igniting the dark.
Each sigh a promise, sweet and true,
A universe births a single spark.

Familiar souls wearing new forms,
Together in every glance.
Through laughter shared and pain endured,
In the chaos, we find our chance.

Time weaves stories, vast and grand,
A tapestry crafted with art.
In the embrace of night and day,
We discover the spark of the heart.

As the constellations shift and sway,
We find solace in the dance.
With every glance, every touch,
A spark ignites, leading romance.

Notes Scribbled in the Margins of Dream

In pages worn, stories lie,
Whispers trapped within the seams.
Thoughts dance lightly, as they sigh,
Notes scribbled in the margins of dreams.

Fleeting moments traced in ink,
Fragments of hopes and silent screams.
In the quiet, we pause and think,
Finding purpose in our schemes.

Chasing visions, we wander far,
Through landscapes of imagination's flight.
Each line a guiding, shimmering star,
Leading us into the night.

Adventures penned with a lover’s quill,
The heart’s narrative takes its shape.
In every fond and distant thrill,
We learn to dream and escape.

So let us write, create our fate,
In margins vast, our hopes redeem.
For every scribble holds some weight,
Notes written in the margins of dream.

Flickers of Hidden Affection

In shadows deep, feelings stir,
A glance exchanged, what might occur.
Whispers soft, in silent nights,
Hearts collide, as time ignites.

Moments stolen, breaths held tight,
Unseen bonds, they take to flight.
Cloaked desires, a tender dance,
In the stillness, a secret chance.

Yet fears linger, doubts arise,
Will they share these hidden sighs?
In quiet glances lost in thought,
A symphony of feelings caught.

Through tangled paths, they find their way,
In fleeting smiles, they'll secretly stay.
Beneath the surface, love is shown,
In every flicker, it's gently grown.

So let the night hold their embrace,
In whispered dreams, they find their place.
For in the dark, affection blooms,
Flickers of light dispel the glooms.

Gravity of the Unmet Eyes

In crowded rooms, two souls collide,
Yet silent gazes cannot confide.
A pull so strong, yet worlds apart,
Gravity holds the beating heart.

Through painted walls, their thoughts collide,
Invisible threads they cannot hide.
Each look exchanged, a moment's grace,
A bittersweet, uncharted space.

Words unsaid weigh heavy like stone,
In silent cries, they feel alone.
Wishes linger on the breath,
Hope entwined with the taste of death.

Paths not taken, dreams unrealized,
In the abyss, their love lies disguised.
Yet still they yearn, through every dare,
To meet the gaze that breaks the air.

What if worlds dared to align?
To break the chains of the divine?
In the dance of the unmet eyes,
They dream aloud as the heart complies.

Lurking Beneath the Surface

A quiet stream holds secrets deep,
Echoes of promises that we keep.
Beneath the flow, the shadows creep,
Emotions buried, time’s dark sweep.

Ripples form from thoughts untold,
In hidden depths, love's stories unfold.
Silent torrents, they rush and churn,
In every corner, lessons learn.

The weight of silence, it can drown,
Yet hopes emerge where fears go down.
In tranquil waters, storms await,
Lurking whispers shape our fate.

What lies beneath that tranquil mask?
An ocean vast, no one would ask.
Through veils of doubt, a light can break,
Truth revealed for connection's sake.

So trust the currents, brave the flow,
For below the calm, true feelings grow.
In layers deep, our hearts reside,
Lurking thoughts that can't subside.

Embracing the Unknown

In the shadow of the twilight's hue,
A world unfolds, both old and new.
Paths uncharted, choices vast,
Embrace the mysteries that hold us fast.

With every step, a breath of light,
In the chaos, we'll find our flight.
Hearts beat louder in the dark,
Trust in the journey, ignite the spark.

Mountains rise and valleys break,
The courage to love, the chance to take.
In the depths of fear, there's beauty found,
In embracing the unknown, we are unbound.

Each twist and turn, an unseen grace,
Life's wild ride, a warm embrace.
Ahead the road may shift and sway,
But in its arms, we'll find our way.

So let us roam, with hearts aglow,
In the realm of what we cannot know.
For in each moment, we come alive,
Embracing the unknown, we truly thrive.

When Curiosity Sparks the Heart

A shadow moves, a glance is caught,
In the quiet corners of thoughts unbought.
Whispers linger, inviting the chase,
Curiosity ignites, filling the space.

Every question poses a brand new dream,
Light filters through, soft and supreme.
Hearts dance to rhythm, a gentle start,
In the mystery sparked, we play our part.

Paths intertwine in the maze of fate,
Understanding grows as we contemplate.
With every turn, we learn to embrace,
The warmth of connection, a tender trace.

The world opens wide, stories unfurl,
In the gaze exchanged, a silent whirl.
With curious hearts, we break apart walls,
Together we rise, as the universe calls.

In the garden of wonder, seeds we sow,
Curiosity's bloom begins to grow.
Together we wander, hearts closely knit,
In the spark that ignites, we find our fit.

Bridges Built on Fleeting Glances

Across the distance, a gaze takes flight,
In the briefest moment, a spark ignites.
Infinite stories concealed in the eyes,
A bridge between souls, where connection lies.

Silent exchanges carry the weight,
Fleeting moments, love's soft bait.
Hearts reach out, though words remain shy,
In the dance of glances, we learn to fly.

Time constricts yet stretches so near,
Each unspoken bond, exquisite and clear.
With every look, foundations are laid,
Bridges of understanding, gently portrayed.

Caught in the rhythm, breaths intertwine,
In the span of a heartbeat, two souls align.
The world around fades, it's just me and you,
In fleeting glances, our dreams come true.

We walk along pathways, mysterious and vast,
Fleeting impressions, like shadows, they last.
Together we build, hand in hand, so brave,
In the quiet moments, our hearts we save.

The Language of Unsung Longings

In whispers of night, desires take flight,
A melody woven in the stillness of light.
Words unspoken, yet vibrant and clear,
Language of longing that only we hear.

Each heartbeat echoes, a story untold,
In the silence shared, our secrets unfold.
With each silent sigh, connections we trace,
In the depths of our souls, we find our place.

The warmth of a touch, a fleeting caress,
In moments of quiet, we learn to confess.
In the shadows of dreams, our spirits entwine,
The language of longing, a love that will shine.

Time stands still as we breathe the same air,
In the heart of the silence, there's nothing to spare.
With every glance, a promise is made,
In the dance of our spirits, true love won't fade.

With every longing, new worlds are spun,
In the tapestry woven, we both become one.
In the language of passion, we find what we seek,
Our unsung longings, poetic and sleek.

Ripples of Unintentional Yearning

In the still waters, emotions collide,
Ripples of yearning we cannot confide.
Unintentional echoes cascade from the heart,
In the quietude lingers, where love plays a part.

Each moment we share sends waves in our souls,
A subtle reminder of uncharted goals.
Though spoken words fail, the silence speaks loud,
In the depths of feeling, we feel so proud.

A glance that lingers, a laugh shared on air,
In the simple moments, a world lays bare.
The tides of connection, in each unplanned sway,
Surfacing feelings that won't fade away.

Between what we say and what goes unspoken,
Lies a longing that leaves each spirit broken.
A flicker of hope in each gesture's embrace,
In the still of the night, we find our grace.

Time dances on, like the leaves in the breeze,
Unintentional yearning brings hearts to their knees.
We ride the ripples, through laughter and tears,
In the depth of these feelings, we conquer our fears.

The Art of Quiet Seduction

In the hush of the night air,
Soft whispers dance like dreams.
Eyes meet in lingering glances,
Unraveled are silent schemes.

Fingers brush, a gentle spark,
Electric between two souls.
Time stands still, hearts race fast,
In this moment, true freedom rolls.

Candlelight flickers softly,
Casting shadows on the wall.
Words are unspoken magic,
In the quiet, we enthrall.

The world fades into stillness,
Just us in this whispered space.
The art of quiet seduction,
Leaves its mark, a sweet embrace.

With every beat, there's an answer,
In the rhythm of our song.
Two bodies finding the cadence,
Where we both truly belong.

A Tapestry Woven with Secrets

Threads of gold and scarlet hue,
Stories linger in the weave.
Whispers echo through the fibers,
In the patterns, we believe.

Each stitch holds a hidden tale,
Secrets spun from years gone by.
Laughter, tears, and whispered dreams,
A tapestry of the sky.

Stitched on hearts and woven tight,
Every knot, a memory's call.
Colors blend in perfect harmony,
Embracing what we find, we fall.

Among the threads, we search for truth,
In the patterns, we discern.
Life's rich fabric, bold and bright,
In our hearts, the secrets burn.

We wear this tapestry with pride,
Shining tales in every glare.
A legacy of love and loss,
Forever woven with great care.

Radiance in the Depths of Shadows

In shadows deep, a light does glow,
Quiet whispers of the night.
Through the darkness, it will flow,
A beacon bold, a guiding light.

Find the beauty in the dim,
Where hopes and dreams begin to gleam.
In the silence, life can swim,
Emerging softly from a dream.

Stars are born in vast abyss,
Their brilliance shines in endless space.
In the dusk, a gentle kiss,
Of warmth and peace, a sweet embrace.

Let the shadows teach us grace,
In the dark, we learn to see.
Radiance within every place,
Filling souls with reverie.

Dancing lights will guide our way,
In the depths, where hearts unite.
Finding joy in every sway,
Radiance is our true delight.

Serendipity in a Strange Embrace

Underneath the starlit sky,
Chance encounters shift our fate.
In a glance, we find a spark,
Magic blossoms, never late.

Windswept paths take us off course,
Yet our hearts embrace the ride.
Fate's designs, a hidden force,
In this moment, we confide.

Laughter shared, eyes wide with wonder,
In the chaos, we align.
Serendipity whispers under,
Guiding us into the divine.

The world spins with a subtle grace,
In random turns, we discover.
A strange embrace, a warm embrace,
In this journey, we recover.

Together, we waltz through the night,
Finding solace in the unknown.
In the serendipity of delight,
A love that feels like home has grown.

Dreamers in the Shadows of Love

In whispers soft, they tread the night,
With hearts aglow, they seek the light.
In shadows deep, their dreams take flight,
A dance of hope, a fleeting sight.

Through tangled paths, their souls align,
A bond unspoken, a secret sign.
In every glance, a spark divine,
In fleeting moments, they intertwine.

Their laughter echoes off the walls,
In silent rooms, true love enthralls.
With every heartbeat, passion calls,
In gentle whispers, their silence falls.

Yet fears may lurk where shadows lie,
Uncertainty makes the spirit sigh.
But in their hearts, they dare to try,
As dreamers rise, they scrape the sky.

Together forged, a tapestry,
Of every wish and memory.
In love's embrace, they'll always be,
Two dreamers lost in harmony.

A Mosaic of Compelling Possibilities

Each tile reflects a vibrant dream,
In colors bright, they start to gleam.
A patchwork of thoughts, a flowing theme,
A dance of fate, a daring scheme.

From shattered hopes, new paths emerge,
In the chaos, visions surge.
A tapestry of life, a gentle urge,
In every fragment, stories merge.

The heart beats loud with every piece,
As whispers of dreams never cease.
Through trials faced, there comes release,
In unity, the soul finds peace.

A canvas born of joy and pain,
In every loss, new strengths retain.
From scattered dreams, the truth remains,
In every heart, a new refrain.

Together we build from shards once lost,
In searching, we find what matters most.
A mosaic rich, at any cost,
In our own hands, the moving gloss.

Flickering Lights in a Dream

In twilight haze, soft lights appear,
They flicker gently, drawing near.
In depths of night, they calm the fear,
A guide through darkness, pure and clear.

With every heartbeat, they pulse and swell,
A symphony of peace, a soothing bell.
In dreams, they whisper a secret spell,
Awakening wonders words can't tell.

Like stars alight in velvet skies,
They twinkle softly, wise and shy.
In fleeting moments, they unify,
A dance of shadows, shooting high.

Yet in their glow, the doubts may creep,
Through tangled thoughts that make us weep.
But still we chase, through realms of sleep,
These flickering lights, our souls to keep.

In every dream, a beacon shines,
Illuminating love's designs.
In waking life, truth intertwines,
As flickers guide us past the pines.

Embracing the Mystery of the Unfamiliar

A world unknown invites our gaze,
In twilight's veil, the darkness plays.
With open hearts, we drift through mazes,
Embracing all life’s tangled phases.

Each whispered word a chance to learn,
In shadows cast, new passions burn.
With every step, our hearts will yearn,
For mystery’s gift, a sweet return.

In paths untraveled, wonders rise,
A dance of fate beneath the skies.
With trust as guide, our spirit flies,
In every challenge, new drives lie.

The strange becomes our closest friend,
In every twist, we’ll find the blend.
Through unknown paths, our hearts will mend,
For every end’s a chance to transcend.

Embracing all that feels so new,
With faith in change, our dreams accrue.
In every moment, clear and true,
The unfamiliar will guide us through.

Emotions that Linger Like Perfume

In a whisper, memories bloom,
Soft petals carried in the room.
Traces of laughter fill the air,
Silent echoes of moments rare.

Fragrant dreams that softly fade,
In twilight hues of love displayed.
Each heartbeat scents the evening's grace,
An essence time cannot erase.

Delicate thoughts like jasmine tease,
A gentle stir upon the breeze.
Infused within the starlit night,
Emotions held in sheer delight.

Through shadows cast by fleeting days,
A symphony of fragrant ways.
Lingering whispers softly cling,
In every scent, a heart will sing.

With every breath, a memory rings,
The dance of love in gentle flings.
Like perfume wafting in the dark,
Emotions linger, leaving mark.

Alluring Shadows in the Light

Beneath the glow of amber skies,
Shadows play where mystery lies.
Dancing figures, soft and shy,
In the twilight, they flit and fly.

Secrets whispered in the dark,
A flicker here, a fleeting spark.
In the light, they twist and twine,
Allure of fate in each design.

Echoes cast from moonlit streams,
Sugared laughter wraps our dreams.
Entwined hearts in soft embrace,
A luminous dance we shall trace.

When shadows merge with gentle glow,
The pulse of night begins to flow.
With every step, a thrill ignites,
In alluring shadows, love invites.

In the silence, stories weave,
A canvas where we dare believe.
Each silhouette, a tale to tell,
In shadows' dance, we find our spell.

The Essence of Unrevealed Passion

Beneath the surface, longing hides,
A tempest where true love abides.
Silent glances, swift and sweet,
In unspoken words, our hearts meet.

Veils of yearning drape our souls,
A secret fire that gently rolls.
In hushed breaths, desire awakes,
With every heartbeat, tension shakes.

Moments linger, draped in night,
Dreams unfurl, hidden from sight.
In paused time, the world stands still,
An essence brewing, hearts to fill.

Layered beneath what words can't say,
Passion's voice finds yet its way.
Wrapped in silence, we await,
The touch of fate, to love create.

Warmth of shadows fills the air,
Every heartbeat, a whispered dare.
In secrets kept, our souls ignites,
Essence of love in whispered nights.

Moonlit Paths of Serendipitous Exchange

On winding roads where starlight glows,
Fate intertwines where sentiment flows.
A chance encounter, hearts collide,
In moonlit whispers, love won't hide.

Each step we take, with stars aligned,
An unplanned joy, uniquely designed.
Captured glances, sweet and shy,
In serendipity, dreams comply.

With every turn, new paths unfold,
Stories shared, in silence bold.
Laughter echoes through the night,
Revealing truth in purest light.

Hand in hand, we roam the dark,
Every heartbeat, a knowing spark.
In this moonlit embrace, we find,
A magic only hearts can bind.

As night surrenders to the dawn,
With dreamers lost but never gone.
In paths we walked, love's thread remains,
In serendipity, joy sustains.

Rooted in the Soil of Enchantment

Beneath the oak, where shadows bend,
Whispers of ancient tales extend.
Roots entwined in the earth's embrace,
Nature's magic, a sacred space.

Moonlit nights with stars in view,
Dreams awaken, fresh as dew.
In this soil, our spirits rise,
Bound to the ground, we touch the skies.

Gentle breezes, sweet and low,
Carrying secrets only they know.
With every tick of time's soft hand,
We grow together, forever stand.

Petals fall like moments shared,
In this garden, love is bared.
Hand in hand through seasons fair,
Rooted deep, a love laid bare.

When storms may come to shake our might,
We'll dance beneath the silver light.
For in this soil, we find our worth,
A bond unbroken, tied to earth.

The Graffiti of Love's Unnoticed Walls

In quiet corners, whispers paint,
Messages of love, shy and faint.
Each stroke a story, bold yet small,
On these walls, our secrets call.

Colors clash in a vibrant dance,
Unseen moments, given a chance.
Hearts entwined in urban sprawls,
Love's graffiti on unseen walls.

Faded echoes of laughter ring,
What joy and sorrow moments bring.
We carve our names on bricks and stone,
In the city's heartbeat, we're not alone.

So many lovers' eyes have met,
In shadows where dreams are set.
These murals tell of lives in thrall,
A canvas bright, the unseen call.

Let the world rush past and ignore,
Our vibrant hearts cry out for more.
In this art of love so free,
We find ourselves, you and me.

The Lure of Untraveled Roads

Lonely pathways, wild and new,
Whispering softly, adventure's due.
Each step leads where dreams may play,
With every turn, the skies turn gray.

Curving lanes through forests deep,
Secrets in shadows, ours to keep.
Stars above guide the way to go,
In lanes untraveled, hearts will glow.

Mountain peaks with snow-capped tips,
Echoes of laughter on wandering trips.
With each horizon, a tale unfolds,
The lure of roads, adventures bold.

Autumn leaves dance ‘neath our tread,
Life's a journey; no need for dread.
Follow the map that heart creates,
On these paths, destiny waits.

So take my hand, we’ll roam away,
Discover the magic of each day.
For in the unknown, we find our truth,
On untraveled roads, reclaim our youth.

Hidden Places where Hearts Meet

In the quiet nooks of twilight's glow,
Where secrets linger, and soft winds blow.
We find each other, in silence deep,
In hidden places, love takes a leap.

Gentle whispers in the starlit air,
Promises linger, a sacred share.
Beneath the boughs of a willow's grace,
Our hearts entwine in this secret space.

Soft petals fall like evening sighs,
In the stillness, our laughter flies.
Time stands still, as moments weave,
In these hidden places, we believe.

A grassy meadow, a stream's embrace,
Where innocence finds a resting place.
In the echo of love, we retreat,
In hidden corners where hearts meet.

So let's return to that sacred ground,
Where our love's melody can be found.
In hidden realms, forever true,
These secret places belong to me and you.

Chasing Echoes of Curiosity

In shadows where whispers dwell,
Flickers of wonder beckon,
Unraveling threads of the unknown,
Adventure calls with a gentle pull.

Every step brings the unexplored,
Each question dances in the air,
The heartbeats synchronize in rhythm,
To the pulse of discovering more.

Through laughter and fleeting sighs,
We chase the light that fades,
Unraveling the mysteries of life,
With each echo that calls us home.

In moments of silence, we listen,
For secrets buried in the ground,
A longing to touch the infinite,
And let curiosity be our guide.

So let us wander, free and bold,
Embrace the journey’s winding path,
For in the chase, we find ourselves,
Lost yet found in the echoes' serenade.

The Aesthetic of Unseen Bonds

In the space between our hearts,
Lie connections that tether us,
Threads woven through the fabric,
Of moments unseen yet felt.

A glance shared across a room,
A smile that speaks more than words,
Subtle gestures; a gentle touch,
Bindings strong, yet quietly held.

In silence, we find our essence,
An understanding beyond the veil,
The soft echoes of companionship,
In the warmth of a steadfast gaze.

Time may challenge our passages,
Yet these bonds stand the test,
In laughter and in sorrow's shade,
A tapestry rich, never frayed.

Let us cherish the unseen ties,
That keep our spirits ever near,
For in these moments, we truly see,
The beauty of what is intertwined.

Vermilion Hues of Silent Desires

Bathed in the glow of twilight's kiss,
Whispers of longing paint the sky,
Crimson dreams pulse in the dusk,
Silent flames yearning to ignite.

Each heartbeat echoes in secret,
Craving the warmth of hidden truths,
Like roses in bloom, we flourish,
Veiled desires, a rich tapestry.

Underneath the veneer of calm,
Passions dance, unseen yet real,
A canvas of vibrant emotions,
Strokes of vermilion and gold.

In shadows, we nurture our hopes,
Breathing life into the unspoken,
As stars align in night's embrace,
Silent whispers ignite the air.

Let us delve into this spectrum,
Where dreams and hearts intertwine,
For in our silent desires,
Lies the essence of what we seek.

Navigating the Currents of Hope

On the river of dreams we float,
Guided by stars in the night,
Each ripple a promise of dawn,
Hope illuminating the way.

With sails billowed by tenacity,
We chart courses of bright tomorrows,
Navigating through shadows and storms,
Trusting the compass of our hearts.

In moments of doubt, we stay anchored,
Roots drawing strength from the earth,
Together, we weather the tempest,
With faith that fuels our journey.

The horizon beckons, golden and wide,
Each dawn a reminder to rise,
In the currents of sheer resilience,
Hope carries us toward the light.

Let us embrace the ever-changing tides,
For in the ebb and flow of life,
We find beauty in the journey,
Navigating with courage and grace.

In the Glow of Ephemeral Moments

In twilight's embrace, we share a glance,
The fleeting spark of a stolen chance.
Whispers of time dance softly near,
In the glow, we hold what we endear.

Moments slip through like sand in hand,
Each heartbeat vital, each second grand.
Captured laughter, a shimmering hue,
Eternalized dreams painted anew.

Stars flicker tales of what we find,
Silent promises etched in the mind.
In gentle shadows, secrets unfold,
In the warmth of now, our story told.

Fleeting hours ignite the night,
Glances turn deep, hearts take flight.
In the silence, an echo survives,
In this glow, our spirit thrives.

As dawn approaches, we shall depart,
But these moments live within the heart.
In memory's embrace, we shall meet again,
In the glow of time, love's eternal reign.

The Pulse of Outer Realms

Beyond the stars, where silence reigns,
The pulse of worlds in distant plains.
Each heartbeat echoes a cosmic song,
In the vastness, we feel we belong.

Nebulae swirl in colors divine,
Galaxies spin in a dance so fine.
Timeless orbits, a mystic flow,
In the pulse of realms, our spirits glow.

Whispers of galaxies, ancient and wise,
Guide us gently through scattered skies.
Cradled in dreams, we drift through space,
In the pulse of the cosmos, we find our place.

Celestial rivers that shimmer and glide,
The magic of starlight, our faithful guide.
In the void, we explore with glee,
In the pulse of the outer, we're wild and free.

As comets streak with a fiery grace,
We embrace the wonders of outer space.
In every heartbeat, the universe gleams,
In the pulse of life, we dance with dreams.

Chronicles of Silent Affections

In the stillness, our stories grow,
Silent whispers only we know.
With every glance, a tale unfolds,
In the chronicles, our heart's gold.

Unspoken words linger in air,
Emotions weave a tapestry rare.
With tender strokes, we paint the night,
In silent affections, hearts take flight.

Moments captured in glances brief,
Laughter shared brings forth relief.
Love's gentle art, a dance so sweet,
In the chronicles, our souls meet.

Through quiet corners, where shadows play,
We find our truth in the softest way.
In every heartbeat, our pulses align,
In silent affections, love's design.

As the moon reflects our secret dreams,
We chase the light, or so it seems.
With every chapter, our journey flows,
In the chronicles, love surely grows.

The Uncharted Territories of Our Hearts

In the wild expanse where feelings roam,
The uncharted lands we call our home.
With every heartbeat, we dare to explore,
Through valleys of longing and oceans of lore.

Winding paths of unspoken quests,
In the shadows, our truth rests.
We navigate through passions unknown,
In these territories, love's seeds are sown.

Meadows of laughter, mountains of grace,
With every step, we find our place.
In the silence, our spirits fly,
In the uncharted, we reach for the sky.

Through storms of doubt and skies so clear,
Our hearts beat strong with nothing to fear.
In every journey, a tale to impart,
In the uncharted, we map our heart.

As twilight descends on the horizon wide,
We cherish the beauty of the heart's ride.
In these lands of passion, we'll always be,
In the uncharted territories, just you and me.

Ethereal Threads that Bind Us

In silence woven, soft and light,
Invisible strands connecting us tight.
Across the miles, through time's embrace,
Love's tapestry glows in every space.

Through laughter shared and sorrow's sighs,
These threads of bonds never tell goodbyes.
In moments captured, joy and pain,
Eternal echoes of our refrain.

With whispers carried on the breeze,
We find our solace in memories.
Each heartbeat syncs, a rhythmic sound,
In this sacred space, we are unbound.

Though shadows dance and fears may loom,
Our connection flourishes, like flowers bloom.
Together we rise as the stars align,
Interwoven fates, together we shine.

Amidst the chaos, we'll not forget,
These ethereal threads, no room for regret.
With faith as our compass, through nights so long,
We nurture the bond that makes us strong.

The Dance of Unspoken Wishes

In the quiet night, dreams take flight,
Hearts whisper secrets, hidden from sight.
Each wish unspoken, yet felt so deep,
In shadows we dance, our souls will keep.

A gentle sway, a celestial tune,
As stars bear witness beneath the moon.
With every glance, our desires align,
In the space between, our worlds entwine.

We yearn for more, yet hold back the truth,
In this silent ballet, we find our youth.
With hope as our guide, we take a chance,
Embracing the night in a timeless dance.

The air is thick with dreams unsaid,
In the rhythm of hearts, we're bravely led.
And though words falter, our spirits soar,
In love's gentle dance, we crave for more.

Through longing glances and tender sighs,
Unspoken wishes, a sweet disguise.
We'll weave our dreams in the stillness bright,
In this dance of wishes, spirits take flight.

In Pursuit of the Unnoticed Flame

Beneath the surface, a flicker glows,
In shadows lingering, passion flows.
A whispered spark, in silence it reigns,
In pursuit of the flame, our heart explains.

Through winding paths and hidden ways,
We search for warmth in the coldest days.
Every glance, a fire waiting to ignite,
In quiet moments, we chase the light.

The world moves fast, but we take our time,
In the hush of night, our spirits climb.
With every heartbeat, we draw near,
To the hidden blaze that holds us dear.

Against the odds, we venture forth,
In the darkness, we find our worth.
Though unseen by many, this flame will grow,
In the pursuit of love, we let it show.

With each passing day, our dreams take flight,
Together we'll fan this timid light.
In pursuit of that which ignites the soul,
We'll keep searching until we are whole.

The Colors of Connection's Canvas

Brush strokes of laughter, hues of delight,
In the gallery of souls, our hearts ignite.
Splashes of sorrow, blending in time,
A masterpiece forged in rhythm and rhyme.

Each moment a color, each joy a shade,
Every bond cherished, never to fade.
In this vibrant dance of life's embrace,
We find our place in the flowing space.

Tints of the past, reflections unfold,
With memories painted in shades of gold.
Together we craft a canvas so wide,
In the frame of connection, we take pride.

Among the textures of joy and pain,
Our hearts create beauty, like sun after rain.
We mix the pigments of laughter and tears,
And celebrate life throughout the years.

With brushes held high, we paint our dreams,
In colors of hope, radiant beams.
Connected we stand, no canvas can part,
For the colors of connection dwell in the heart.

Dreamscapes Silhouetted in Charm

In twilight whispers, dreams ignite,
Silhouettes dancing in soft moonlight.
A canvas painted with gentle hues,
Where laughter lingers, and hope renews.

Stars twinkle softly, secrets shared,
In this enchanting world, we're ensnared.
With every heartbeat, magic unfolds,
As stories of wonder are lovingly told.

The breeze carries wishes, ever so sweet,
In dreamscapes where time and space meet.
Moments of bliss in the quiet night,
We chase the shadows, our hearts take flight.

Together we wander, hand in hand,
Through realms of dreams, a vast wonderland.
In the embrace of the night's tender sigh,
We find our solace as echoes reply.

Awake, yet enchanted, lost in this trance,
Dreamscapes beckon us into their dance.
With every breath, the charm reappears,
In twilight's embrace, we conquer our fears.

Allure under the Moon's Caress

Beneath the glow of the silvery light,
Whispers of secrets wrap the night tight.
The world transforms, soft and divine,
Drawn together by an unseen line.

In shadows, our dreams break free,
Twinkling stars, our only decree.
The moon's caress, a lover's touch,
With every heartbeat, we crave it much.

Mysteries linger in the gentle breeze,
Inviting us closer, urging to seize.
Each moment crafted, each glance a spark,
Guided by heavens, igniting the dark.

Time stands still in this tender glow,
As emotions weave in a rhythmic flow.
Surrendered hearts, no need to impress,
Allure surrounds us in nature's dress.

Bound by the magic of this sweet night,
Held in its embrace, everything feels right.
Together we linger, the world fades away,
In the moon's caress, we wish to stay.

A Journey through Unfamiliar Landscapes

On paths uncharted, we boldly roam,
Through valleys of green, where wildflowers comb.
With every step, the heart learns to sing,
A journey begins, new magic we bring.

Mountains rise high, veiled in the mist,
An echo of dreams, too bold to resist.
The rivers chat softly, guiding our way,
In the twilight hues of the closing day.

Each turn of the road reveals another sight,
A tapestry woven with morning light.
In silence, the trees whisper tales of yore,
As nature unfolds what we'd longed to explore.

The horizon stretches, inviting our gaze,
Coloring moments in vibrant displays.
In every landscape, a story awakes,
An invitation to dance, in life's gentle shakes.

Lost in the wonder, we find ourselves free,
In this realm of enchantment, just you and me.
Where memories blossom, and spirits collide,
We journey together, hearts open wide.

Between the Lines of Chemistry

In whispers of science, secrets unfold,
Atoms collide where hearts grow bold.
Between the lines, a spark ignites,
Crafting connections in shadowed nights.

Molecules dancing, a waltz so rare,
Bound by attraction, a vibrant affair.
In the lab of love, equations align,
With every reaction, our fates entwine.

The universe whispers in frequencies low,
As we navigate tides with a rhythmic flow.
With every heartbeat, a pulse we feel,
Between the equations, love becomes real.

In the silence of moments, alchemy stirs,
Transforming the mundane as passion occurs.
Beneath the surface, our chemistry thrives,
Drawing us closer, where magic derives.

So here we stand, between science and art,
A harmonic blend of souls, never apart.
In the dance of creation, our spirits fly,
Between the lines, together we lie.

The Allure of the Unreachable

In shadows where whispers dwell,
Dreams linger, a distant bell.
Stars twinkle with secret grace,
Guiding hearts to a hidden place.

A horizon beckons, wise and wide,
Yet distance swells with every stride.
We chase the mirage, hearts in flight,
Lost in the beauty of fading light.

The mind dances in curious flight,
While hands extend, grasping the night.
Each spark ignites a fierce desire,
To reach the sun, to touch the fire.

Time eludes like a fleeting glance,
In the twilight's soft, enchanting dance.
We long for what we cannot hold,
Stories untold, dreams of gold.

Yet in the chase, there lies our truth,
The beauty found in the uncouth.
For every step we cannot claim,
Adds to the essence of the flame.

Fleeting Moments of Uncertainty

In the hush before the dawn,
Questions linger, like a pawn.
Every breath, a whispered doubt,
Unraveling what life's about.

A glance that flickers, swiftly fades,
In the dance of the masquerades.
Time weaves tales of what's to be,
Yet uncertainty sets us free.

Moments seem to twist and swirl,
Like leaves caught in an autumn whirl.
We dare to leap into the unknown,
Finding solace in seeds we've sown.

A heartbeat echoes, rapid pace,
As choices flicker, a fleeting trace.
We ride the waves, unsure and bold,
In the wake, our stories unfold.

In every tremor, a spark ignites,
The beauty thrives in fleeting nights.
Uncertainty's song, a soft refrain,
Leads our hearts through joy and pain.

The Warmth of Subtle Approaches

In the silence before a touch,
Gentle smiles say so much.
Eyes meet in a fleeting glance,
Inviting souls to dare to dance.

Words linger softly on the air,
Each syllable crafted with care.
A warmth brews in the quiet space,
Drawing hearts to a tender place.

With every breath, connection grows,
Like a garden that quietly glows.
In the pause between, secrets unfold,
Promises whisper, tales retold.

Subtle touches, echoes of grace,
Bringing hearts to a sacred space.
In the stillness, we find our place,
Time slows down in a warm embrace.

Treasured moments, fleeting yet bright,
Illuminate the depths of the night.
With every heartbeat, we come alive,
In the warmth of love, we all thrive.

Encountering the Unfamiliar Flame

A spark ignites in the deep unknown,
Where shadows flicker and courage's grown.
In uncharted lands, we find our way,
Chasing the dawn of a brand new day.

With every step, the fear subsides,
As bold hearts venture where magic hides.
Embracing chaos, we start to see,
The beauty woven in mystery.

A flame that dances, wild and free,
Sparks of passion ignite the sea.
With every glance, our worlds collide,
Drawing closer, swept by the tide.

In the heat, we break our chains,
Finding freedom that love sustains.
The unfamiliar becomes our guide,
In the warmth, we shall abide.

Each flicker a promise, a call to ignite,
In this journey, we embrace the night.
For in the unknown, we uncover our names,
In encountering the unfamiliar flames.

Chasing Echoes in Stillness

In quiet woods where shadows play,
The whispers of the past hold sway.
Echoes linger, soft and low,
In stillness, secrets gently flow.

Beneath the boughs, the silence sings,
Of dreams and hopes, of fleeting things.
We chase the echoes, hearts in tune,
Guided by the silver moon.

Each step we take, a breath we draw,
In nature's grasp, we find the law.
The echoes dance, both near and far,
In stillness, we become a star.

Embrace the quiet, feel the space,
Where every heartbeat leaves a trace.
In chasing echoes, we find peace,
A timeless moment that won't cease.

Where Hearts Dance to Unknown Rhythms

In twilight's glow, the night awakes,
With whispers soft, the silence shakes.
Hearts in rhythm, lost in grace,
In shadows, find our sacred space.

With each heartbeat, we drift and sway,
In the tapestry of night and day.
Unknown melodies fill the air,
As souls entwine without a care.

We dance on dreams, on hopes alight,
In vibrant hues of endless night.
Each twirl a promise, each spin a vow,
In this wild waltz, we anchor now.

The world dissolves, a fleeting glance,
In this moment, we take a chance.
With hearts as one, the unknown calls,
Where love prevails and fear dissolves.

The Alchemy of Unbidden Companionship

In chance encounters, souls collide,
Where laughter flows and hearts confide.
Unbidden friends, a spark ignites,
In every word, our spirit lights.

Through shared stories, our paths entwine,
A bond unspoken, yet divine.
In silence shared, a treasure found,
In every glance, a love profound.

We wander through the shifting tides,
With arms wide open, hearts as guides.
The alchemy of trust unsealed,
In every moment, fate revealed.

Together we laugh, together we cry,
In our companionship, we learn to fly.
Each fleeting moment becomes a gem,
In unbidden friendship, we find our hem.

Winds of Connection Whispering Softly

The winds weave tales through branches high,
With every breath, they gently sigh.
Connection's warmth, a tender breeze,
In whispering echoes, hearts at ease.

As leaves embrace the sky’s soft hue,
In every gust, I think of you.
These winds convey what words can't say,
In twilight’s glow, they softly play.

The currents dance, entwined as one,
In every breath, a story spun.
Winds of connection, sweet and clear,
Whispering love that draws us near.

Together, we sail on breezy threads,
In every heartbeat, magic spreads.
Through gusts of change, we find our way,
In winds of connection, we choose to stay.

In the Realm of Unuttered Feelings

Silent whispers drift through the night,
Carried on the wings of dreams bright.
Words unspoken linger in the air,
A dance of emotions, fragile and rare.

Glimmers of hope in shadows cast,
Moments fleeting, too precious to last.
Hearts entwined yet worlds apart,
In the silence, we hide our heart.

The moon listens to secrets we keep,
In twilight's embrace, where shadows creep.
An echo of longing, a sigh in the breeze,
Unraveled threads woven with ease.

Beneath the stars, our gazes collide,
In the depths of silence, we find our guide.
A tapestry woven with unspoken grace,
In this realm, we find our place.

Fleeting moments, like mist in the dawn,
Glance after glance, an unbroken bond.
In the realm where feelings remain,
We discover the beauty in unvoiced pain.

The Glow of Unexpected Affinity

In a crowded room, your eyes meet mine,
A spark ignites, a moment so fine.
An unseen force pulling us near,
In every glance, everything's clear.

Laughter spills like sunlight's embrace,
In this connection, we find our space.
Time stands still with every shared smile,
With thoughts entwined, we linger awhile.

Echoes of laughter dance in the air,
A bond so deep, so delightfully rare.
In unexpected moments, joy comes alive,
In this sweet glow, our spirits thrive.

With every heartbeat, a rhythm anew,
The world fades away, just me and you.
In this unexpected affinity we find,
A timeless connection, forever entwined.

Through the chaos, we navigate grace,
In this warm glow, we find our place.
An invitation to wander the skies,
In the light of our bond, uncertainty dies.

The Enchantment of Unfurling Hearts

In twilight's glow, our secrets unfold,
Tales of dreams that were never told.
With every heartbeat, we weave our art,
In the enchantment of unfurling hearts.

Petals of trust gently unfurl,
In this shared space, our emotions swirl.
With tender caresses, strong and kind,
We lose ourselves, leaving worries behind.

A symphony blooms in the silence we share,
With the fragrance of hope filling the air.
In the garden of feelings, wild and free,
Every moment, a cherished memory.

Our laughter dances, a melodic tune,
Under the spell of a silver moon.
As our stories entwine in the gentle night,
In the enchantment, we find our light.

With courage, we blossom, no fear in sight,
In this embrace, everything feels right.
Together we stand, two souls in accord,
In the magic of love, our hearts are restored.

The Veil of Hidden Draw

Behind closed doors, a secret glows,
An unspoken bond that gently flows.
Though words are few, the feelings soar,
In the veiled whispers, we seek for more.

A glance exchanged, electric and bright,
Awakens something deep in the night.
In heartbeats synchronized, we find our call,
In the hidden draw, we surrender it all.

Like shadows dancing in candlelight,
In the depth of silence, we feel so right.
With every breath, a promise unmade,
In the veil of connection, love will cascade.

Each stolen moment a treasure unveiled,
In this maze of feelings, we've never failed.
With layers concealed, the truth finds a way,
In the hidden draw where souls sway.

In this quiet space, we bloom and thrive,
With passion ignited, our spirits alive.
An unending journey where dreams intertwine,
In the veil of hidden draw, love's design.

Printed in the USA
CPSIA information can be obtained
at www.ICGtesting.com
LVHW022026311024
795321LV00003B/55

9 789916 890318